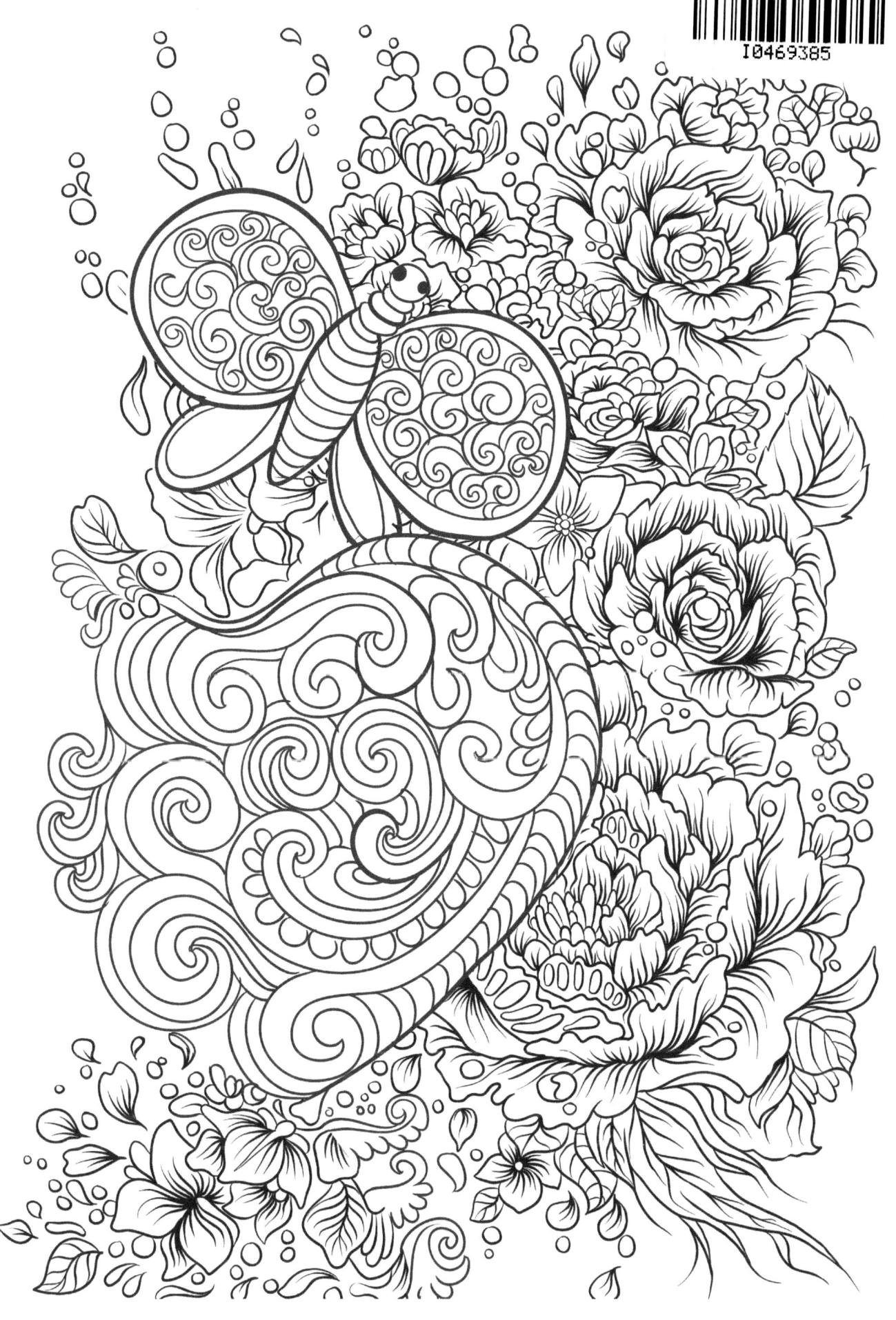

Download your PDF version for easy printout:

A link to an Adobe PDF version of this book is available at the end of this book. It contains high resolution images for you to print out on paper. It's instantly accessible after your book purchase.

ISBN: 978-1523703708
Copyrights © 2016 All rights reserved
by: Adult Coloring Book Sets
Illustrated by:
Mandala & Caricature Illustration
Joshua Lazana Lagman and Jade Villaremo

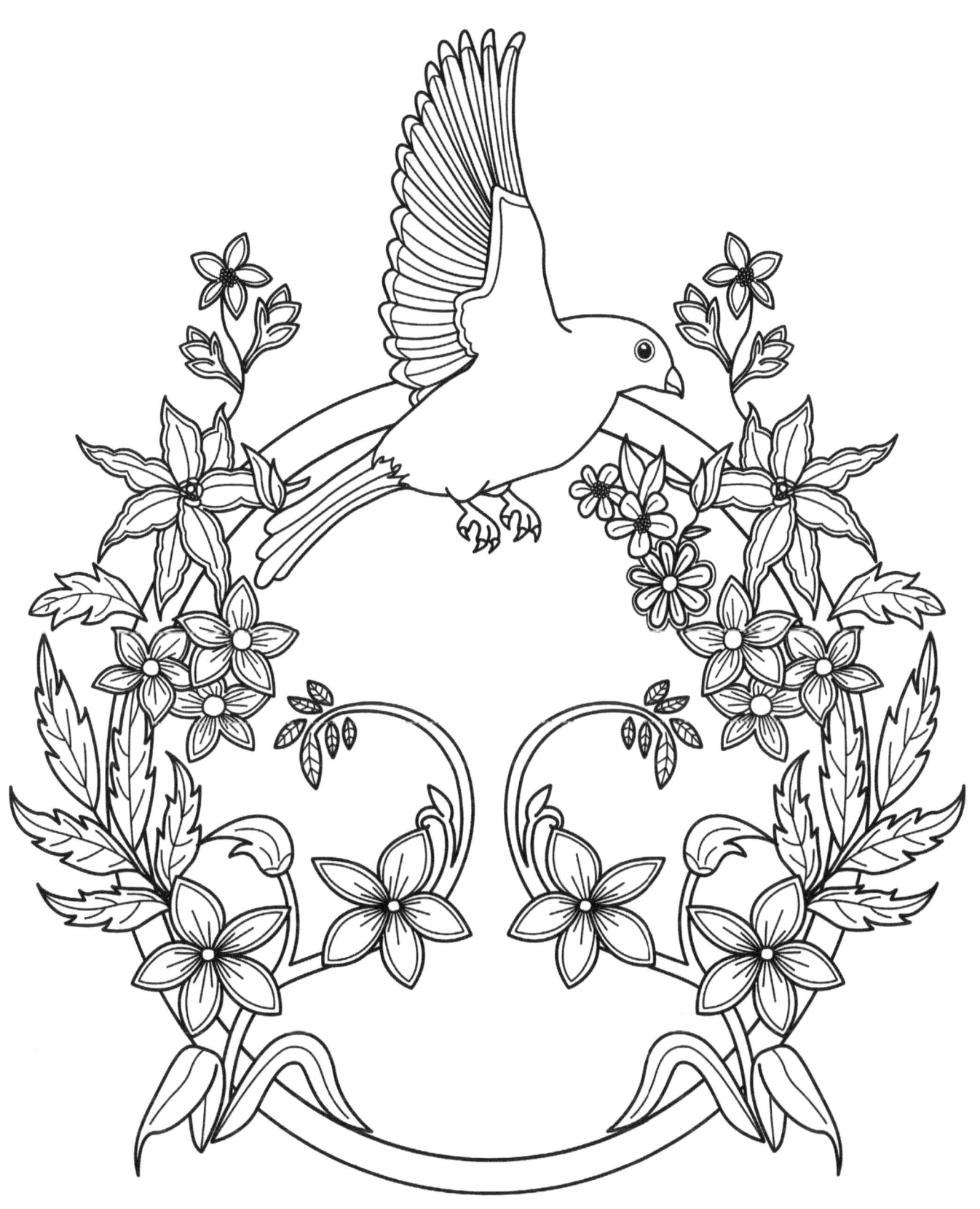

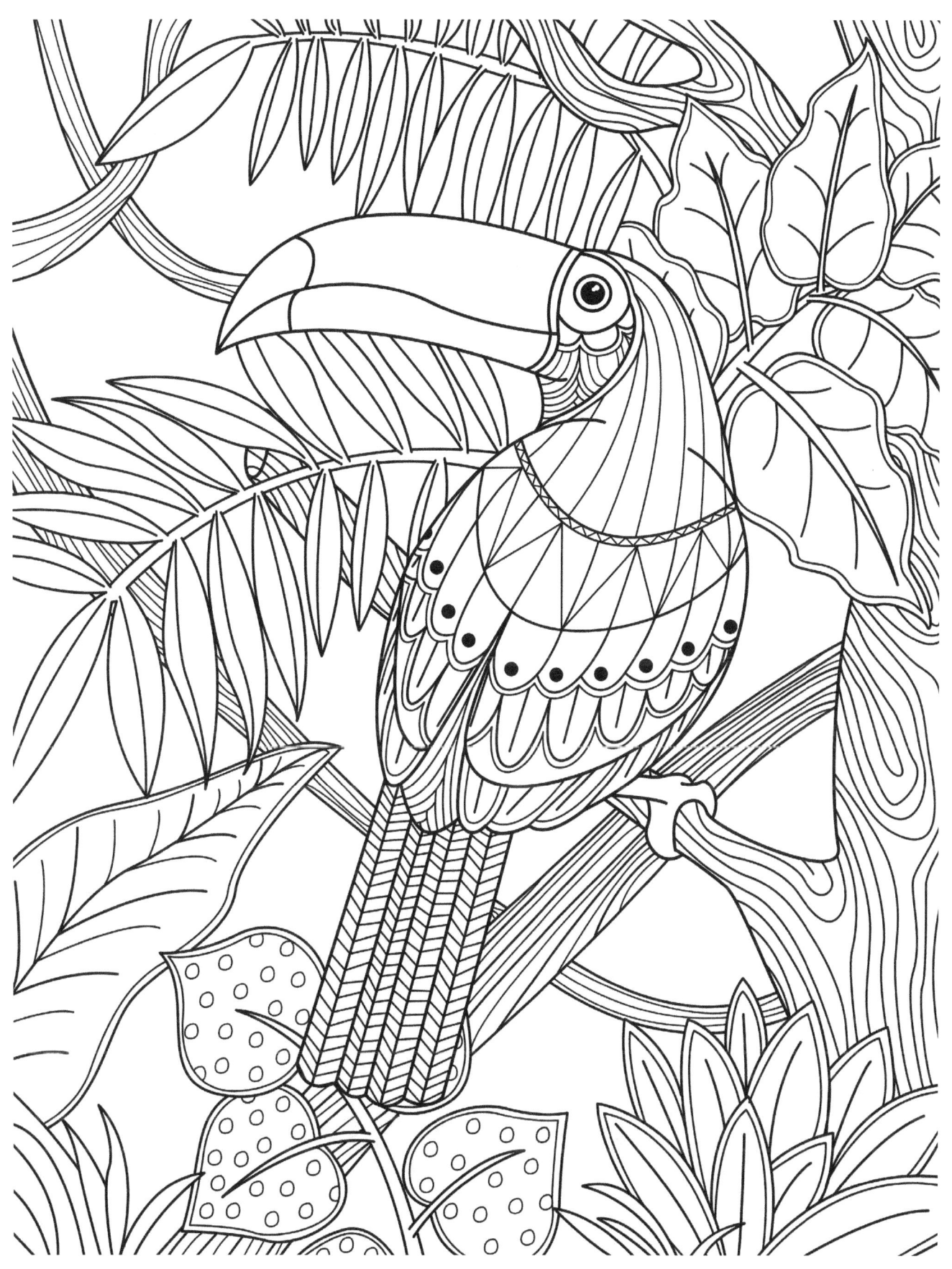

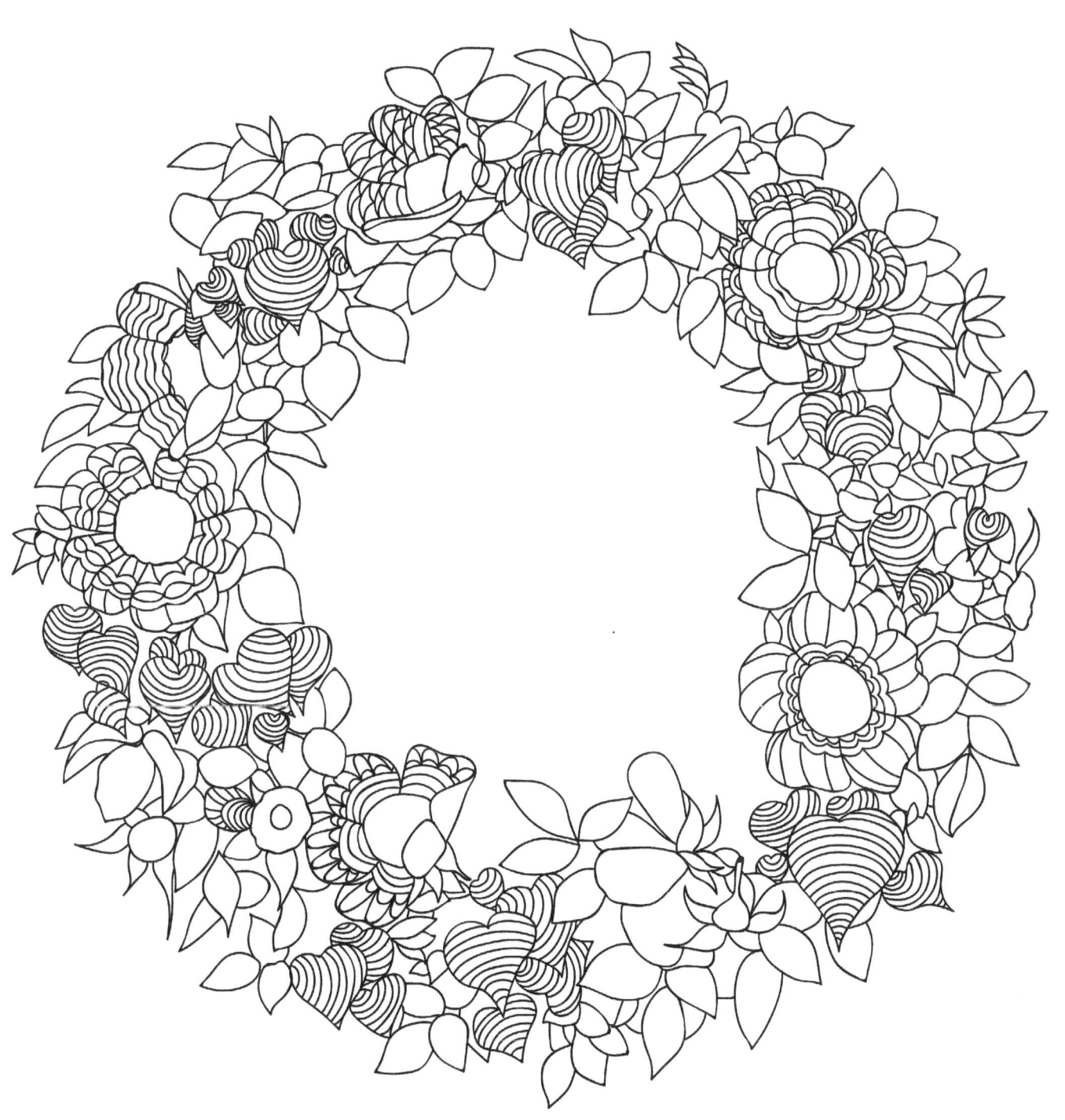

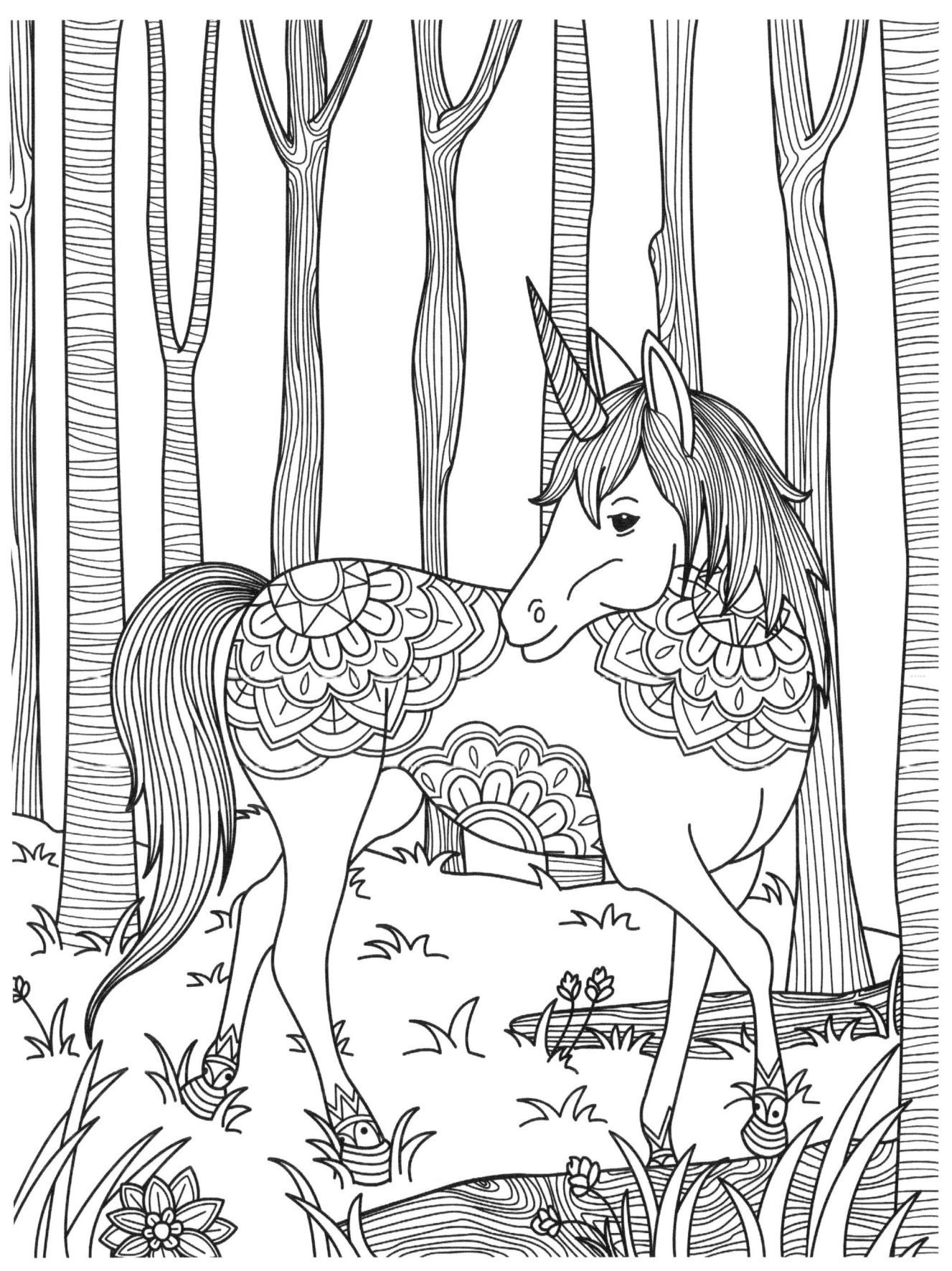

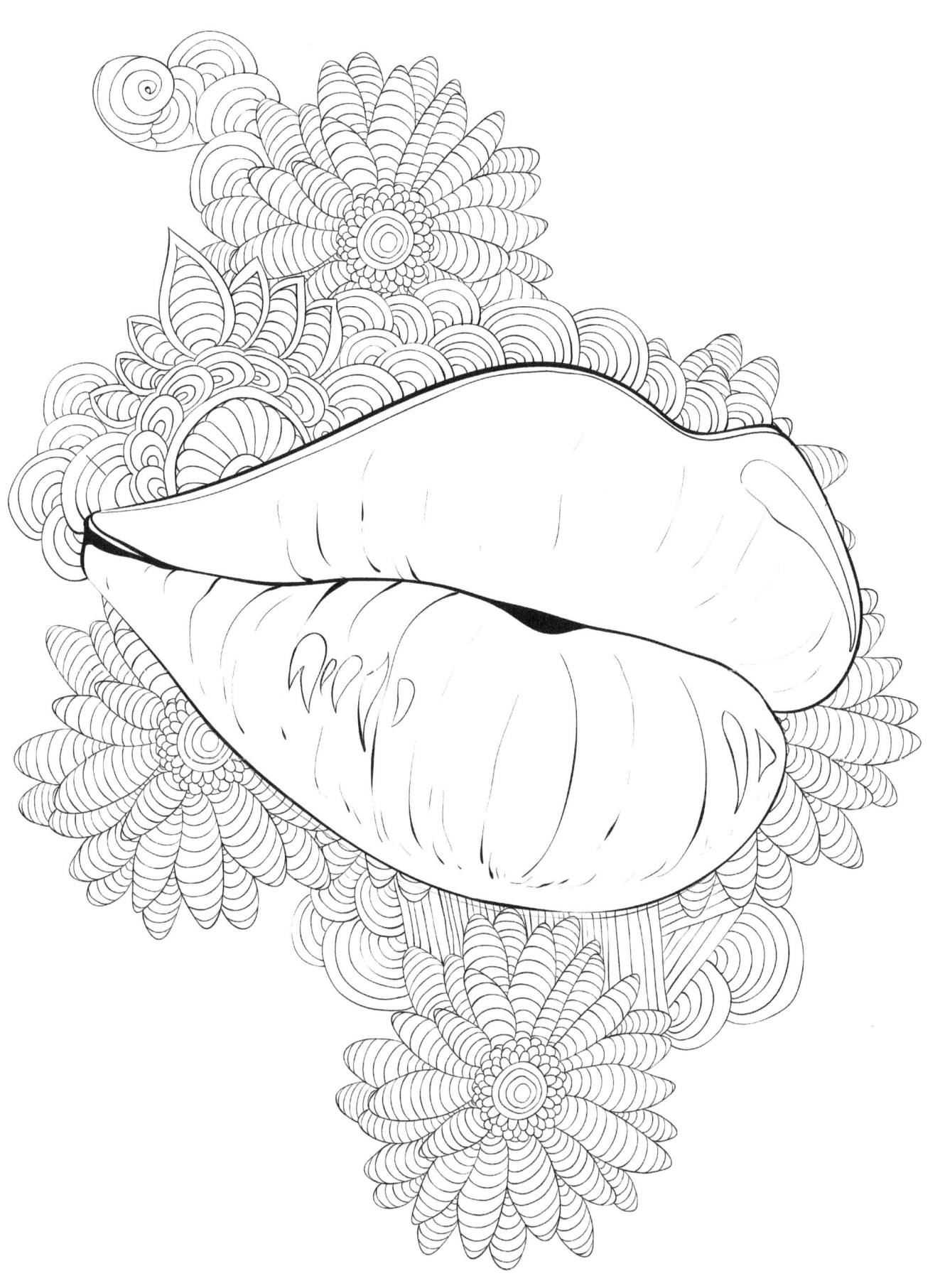

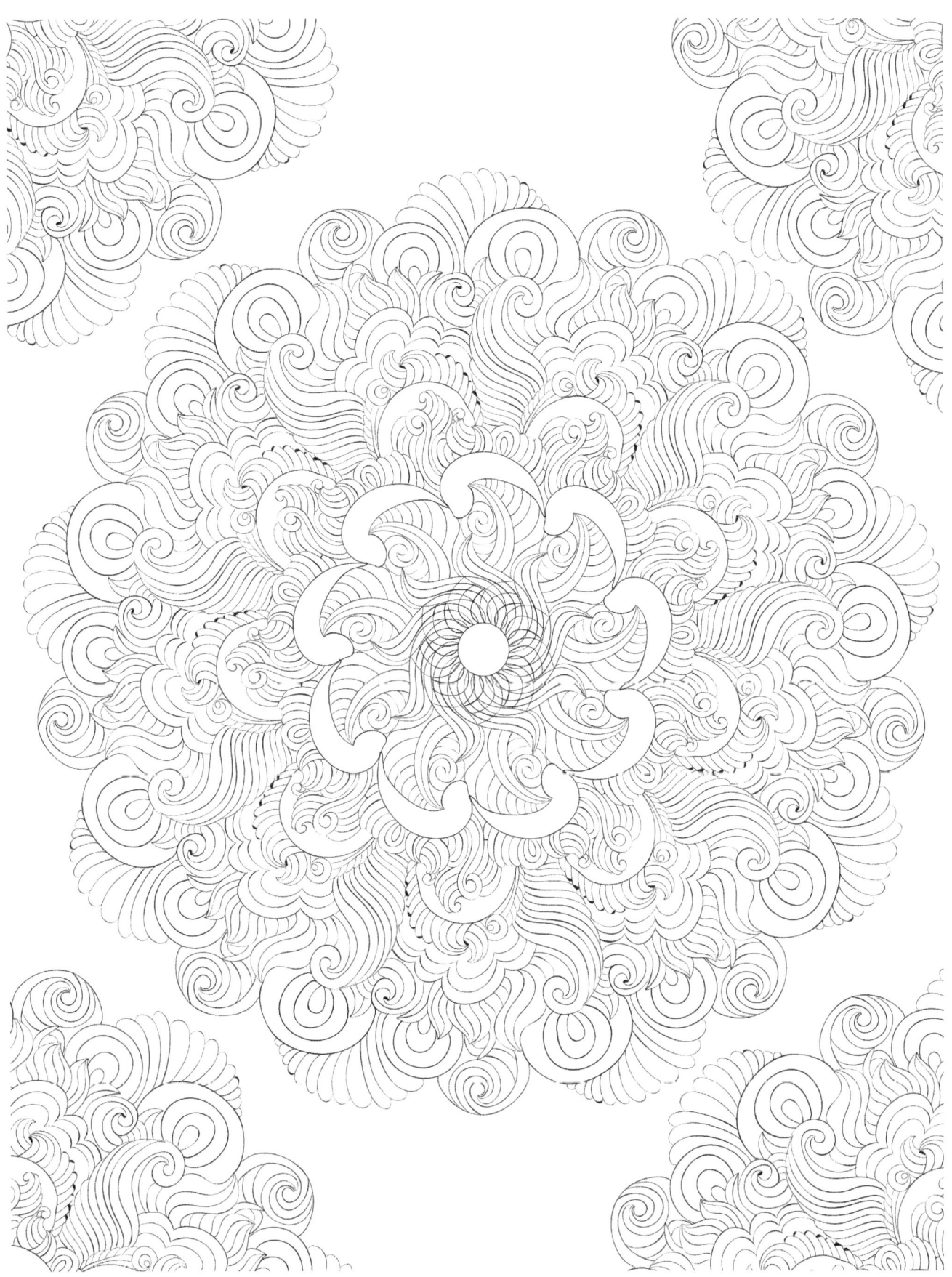

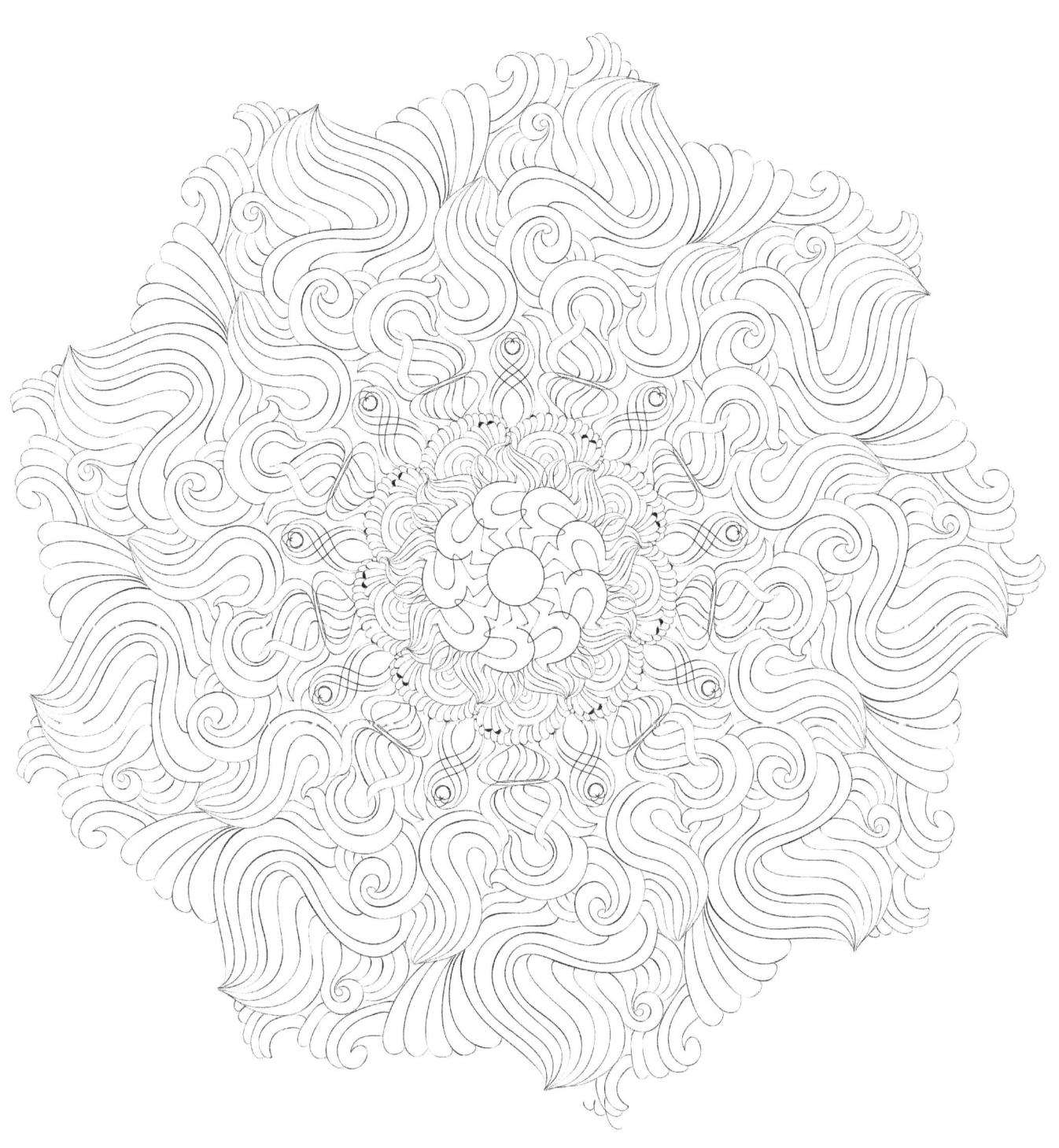

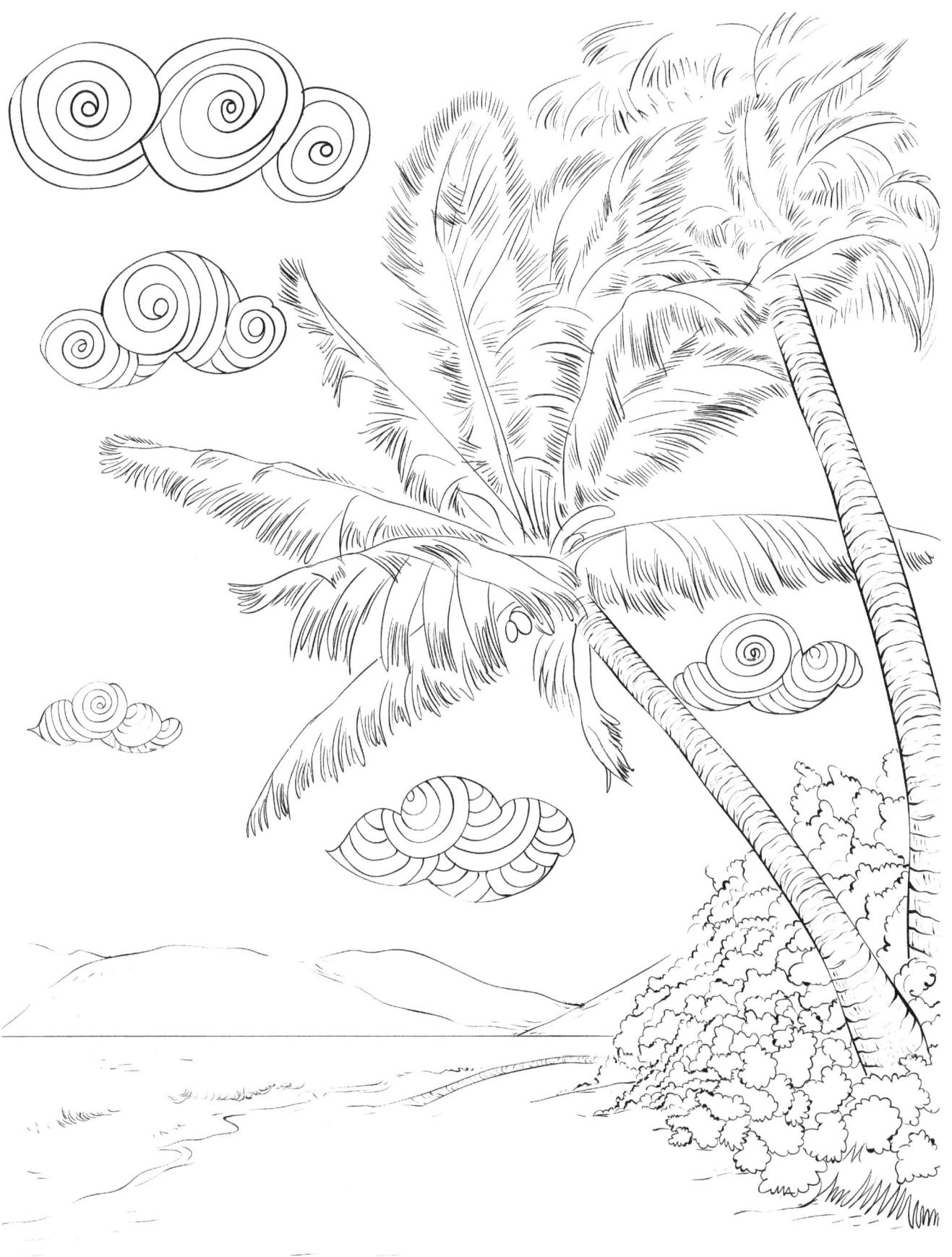

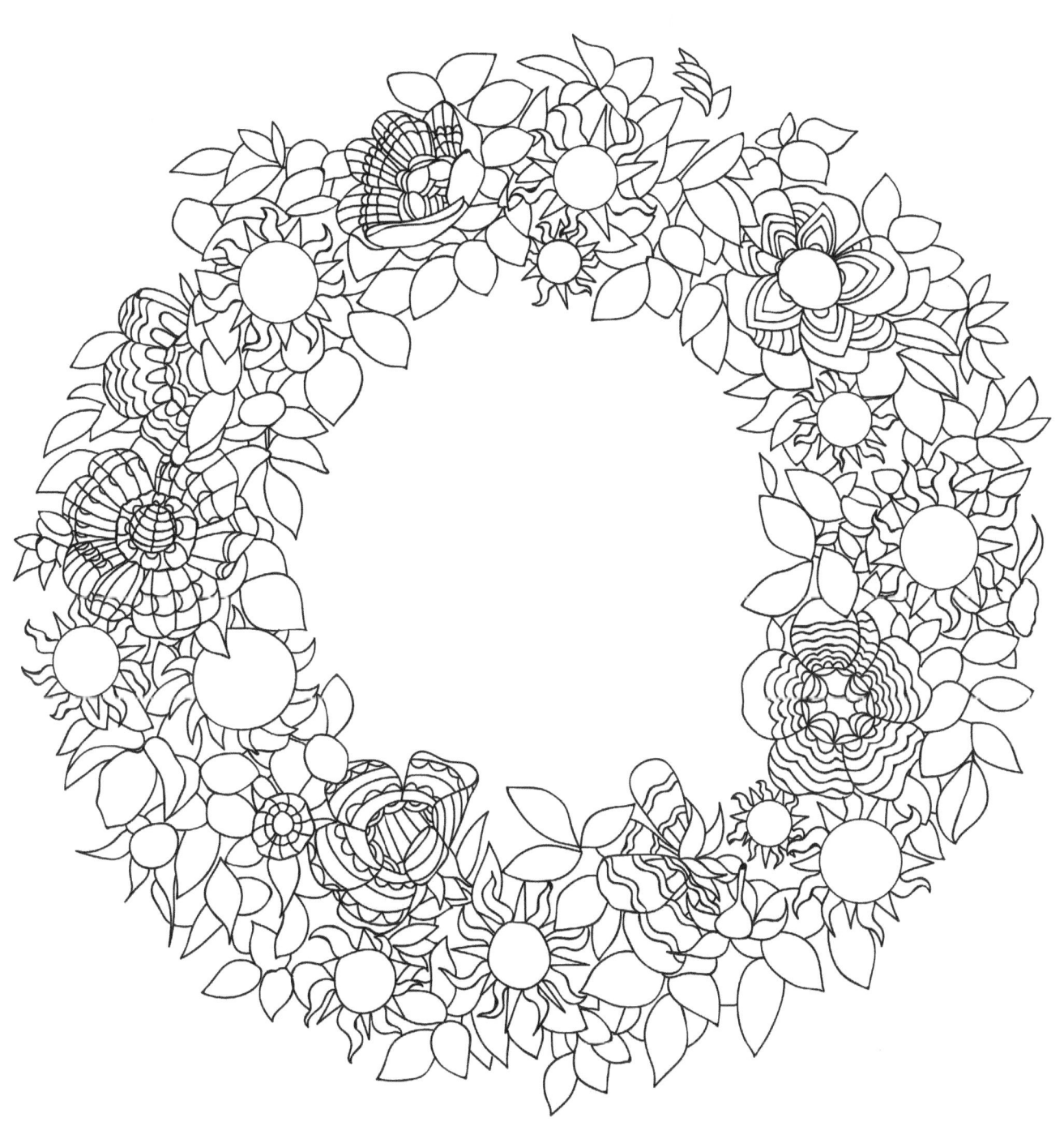

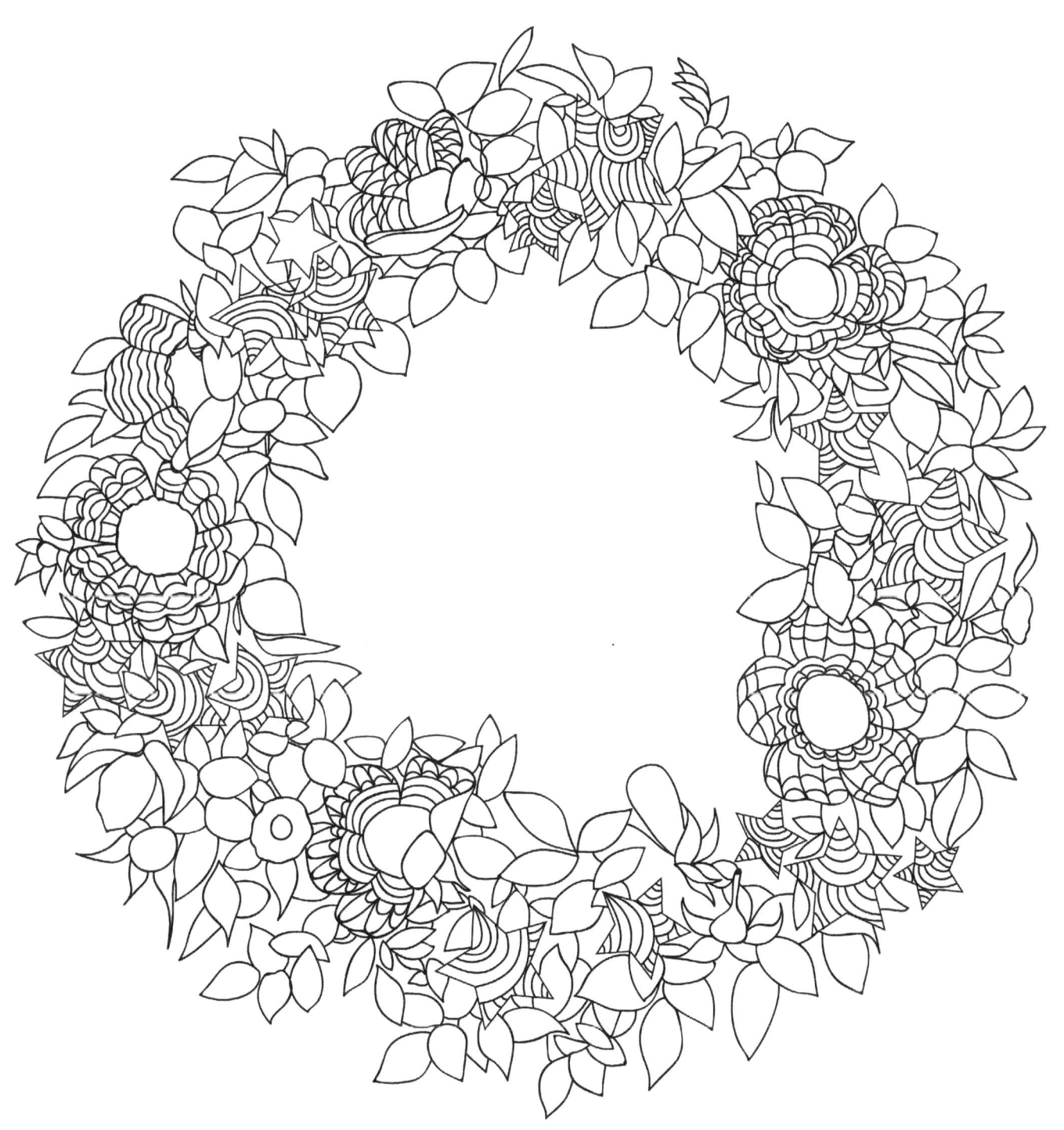

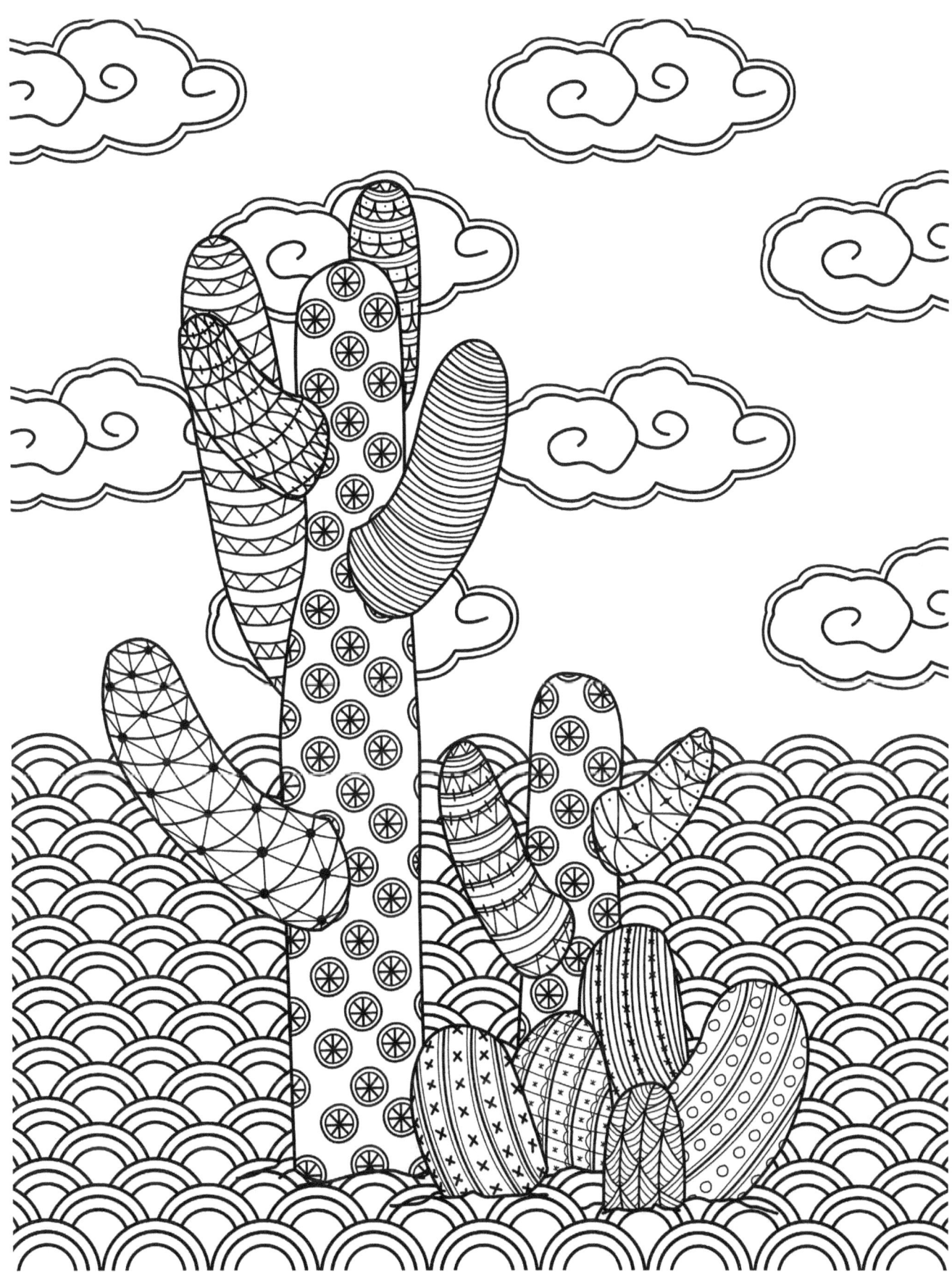

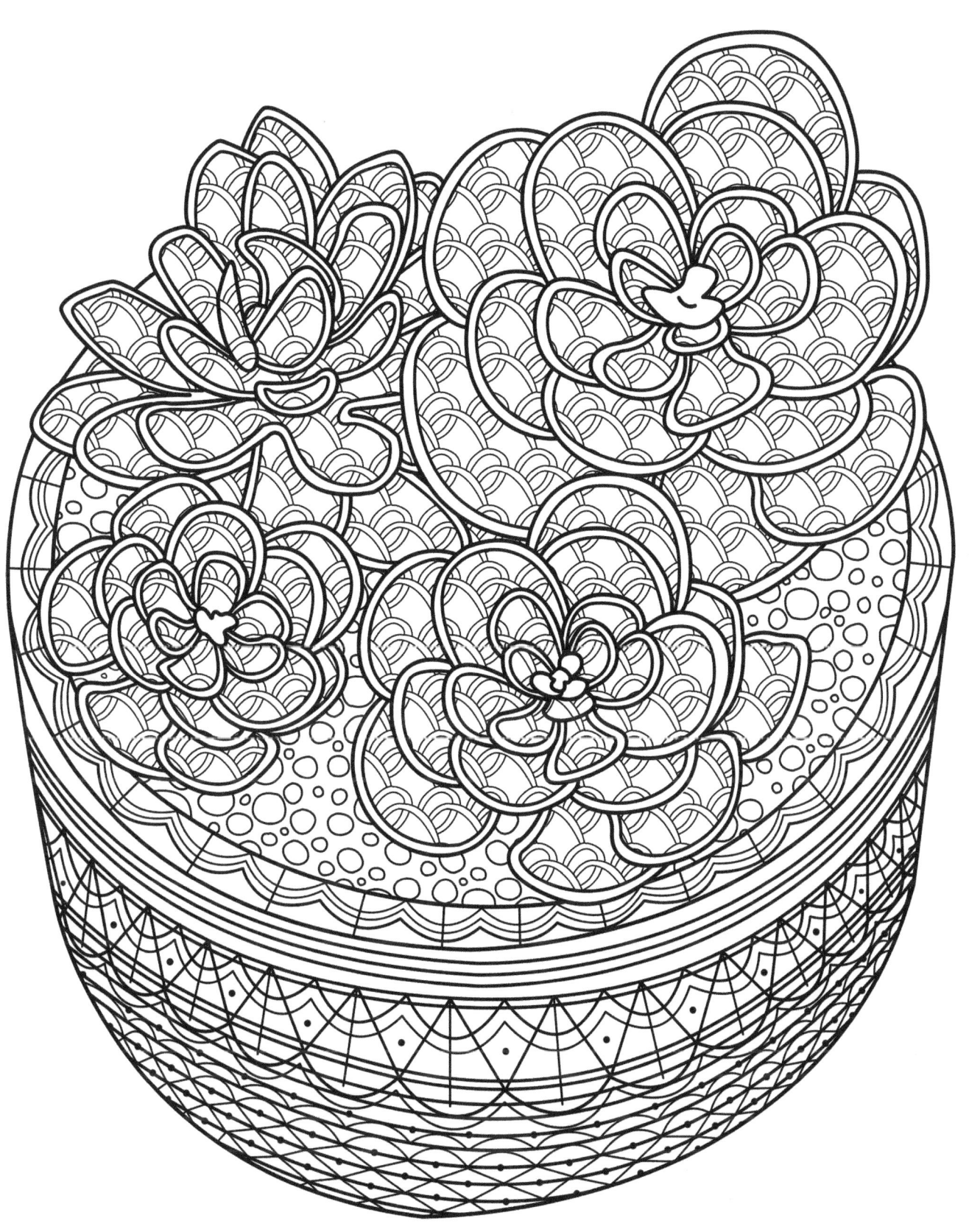

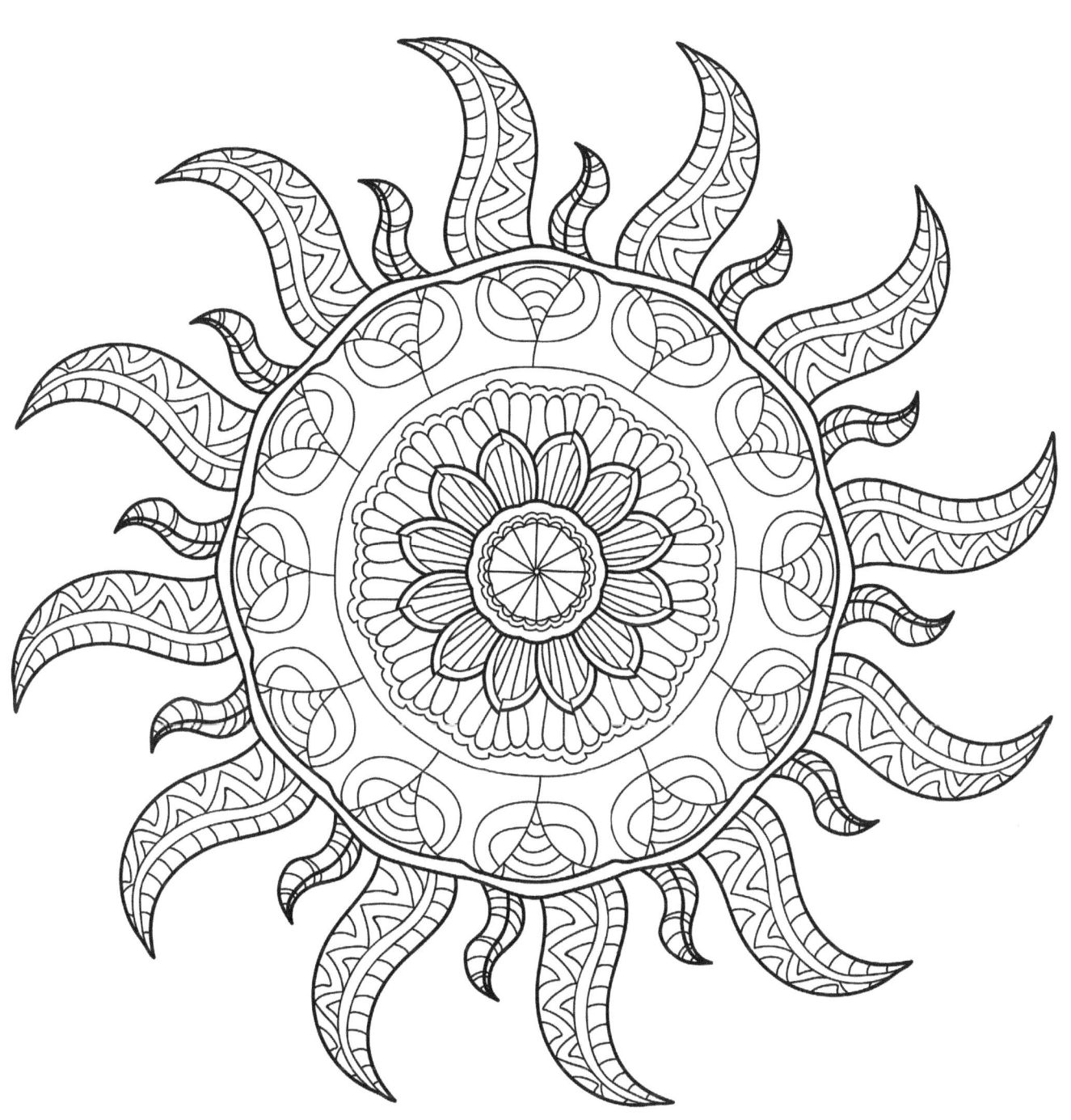

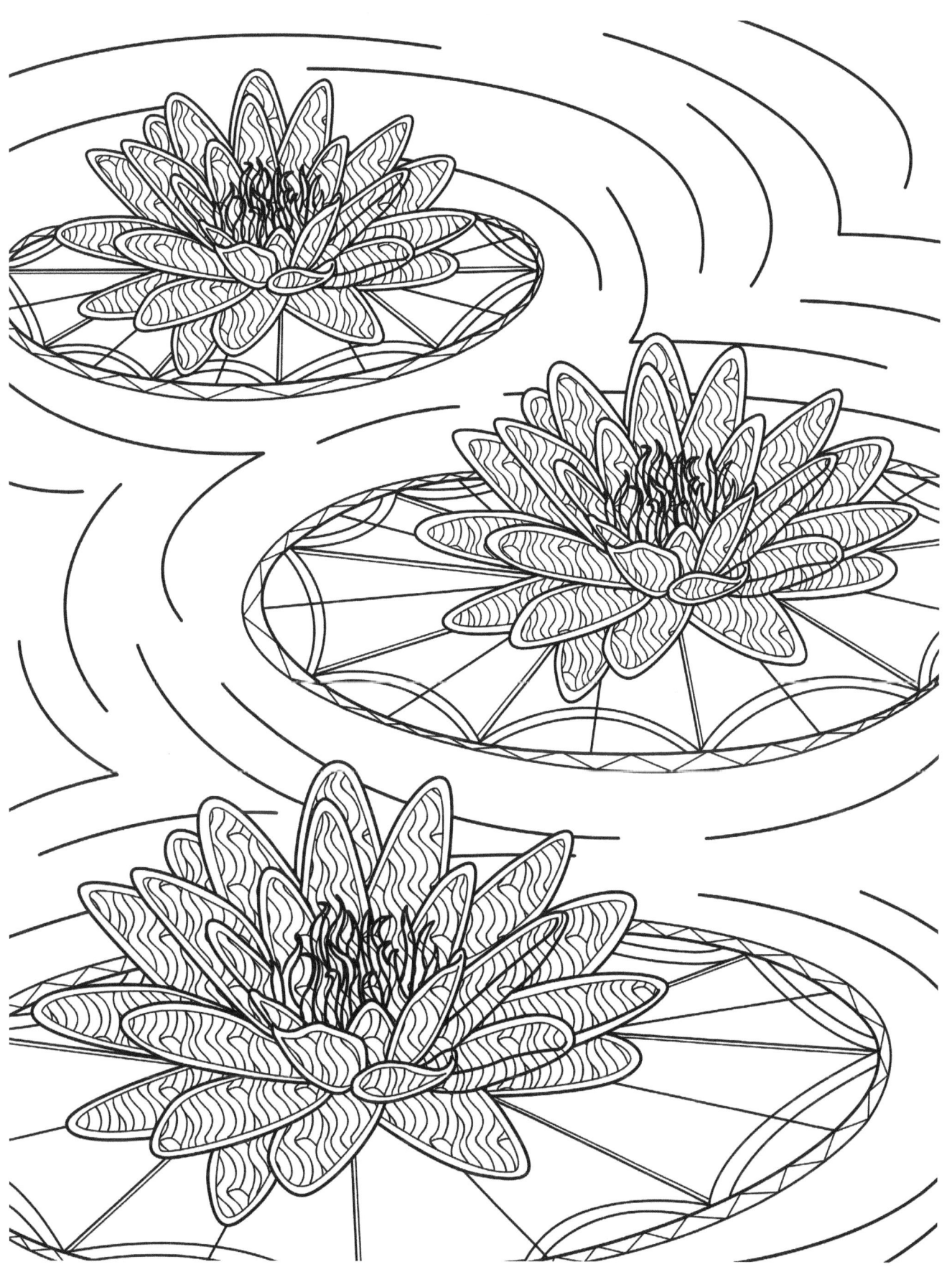

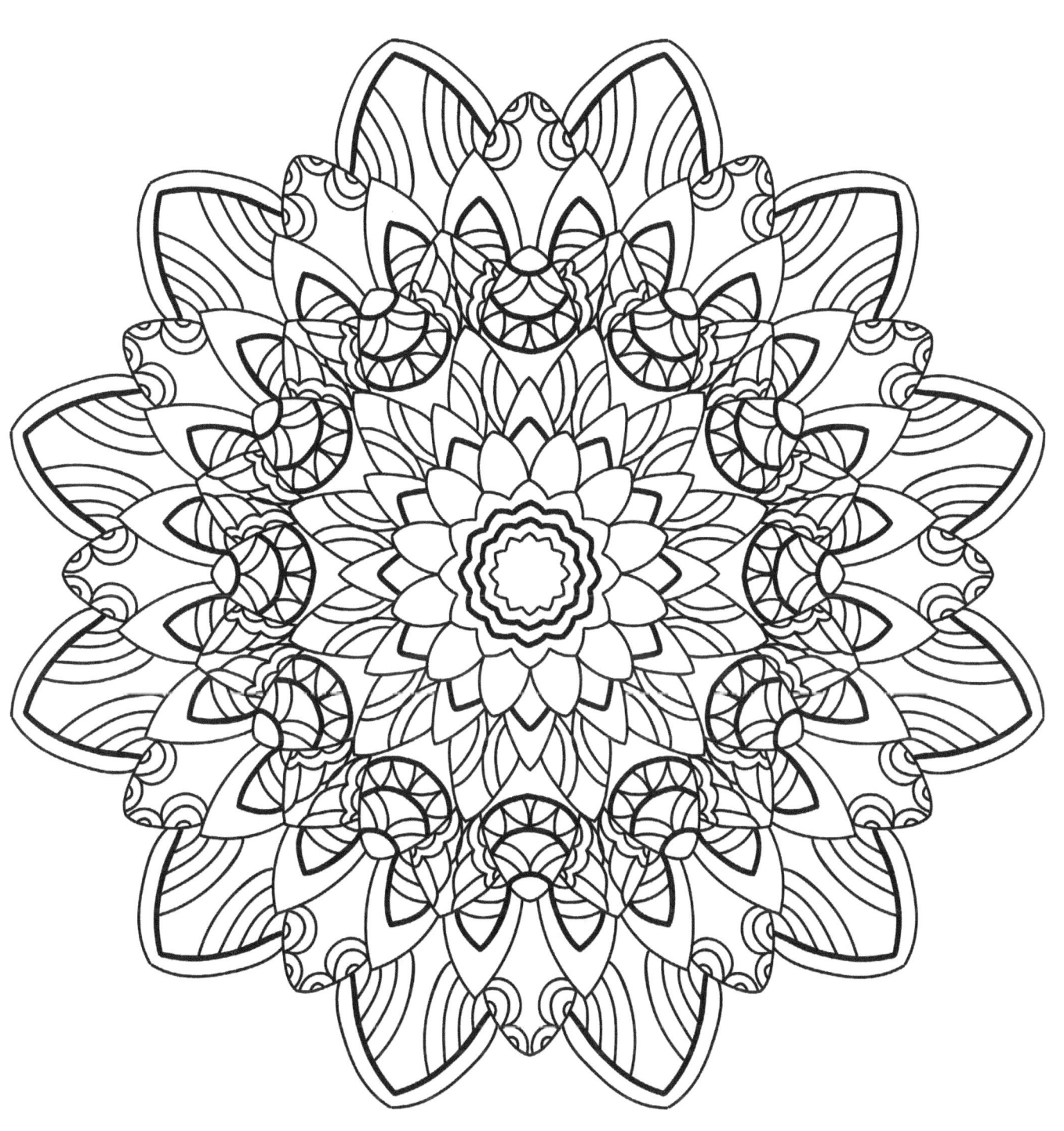

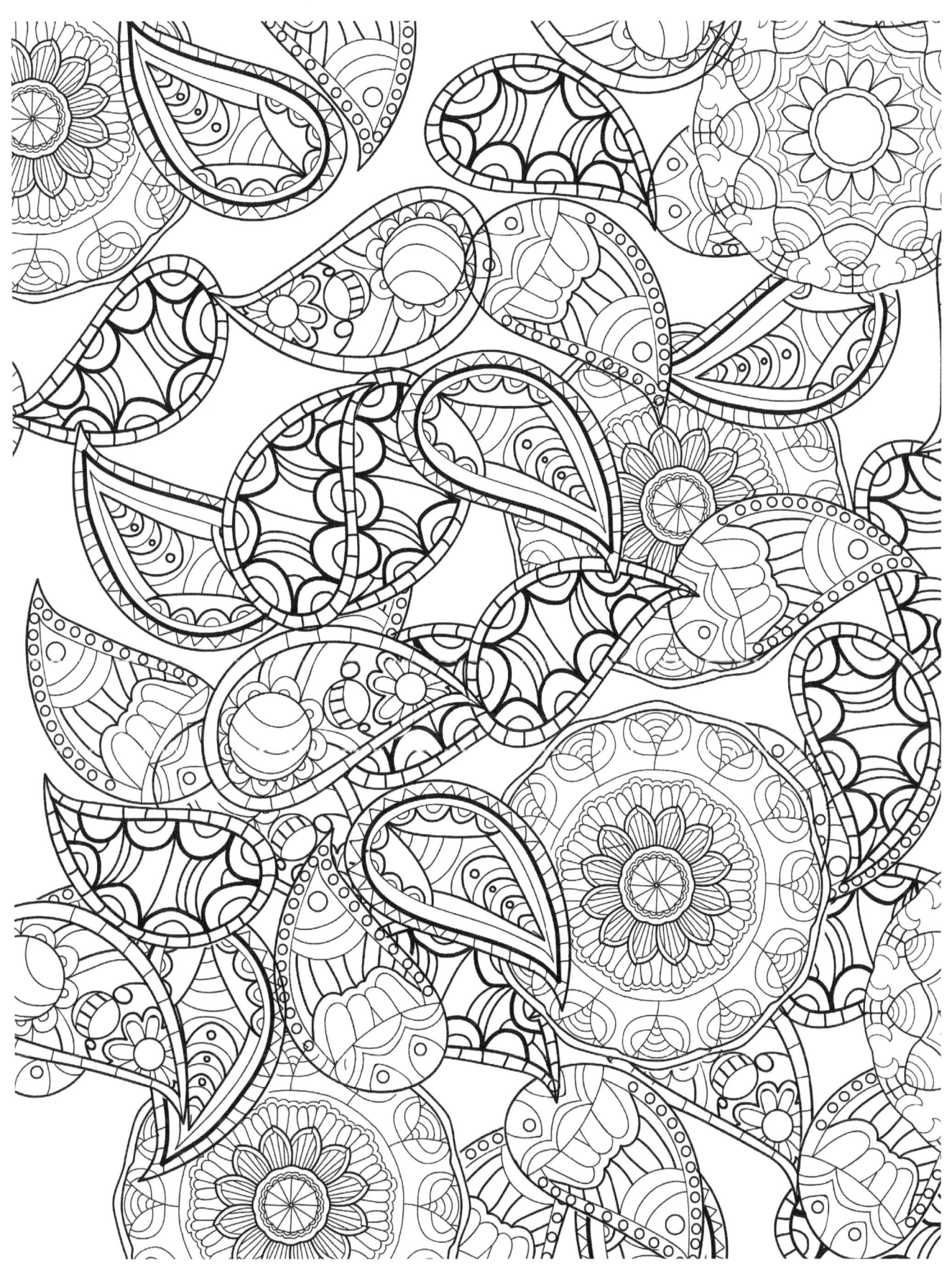

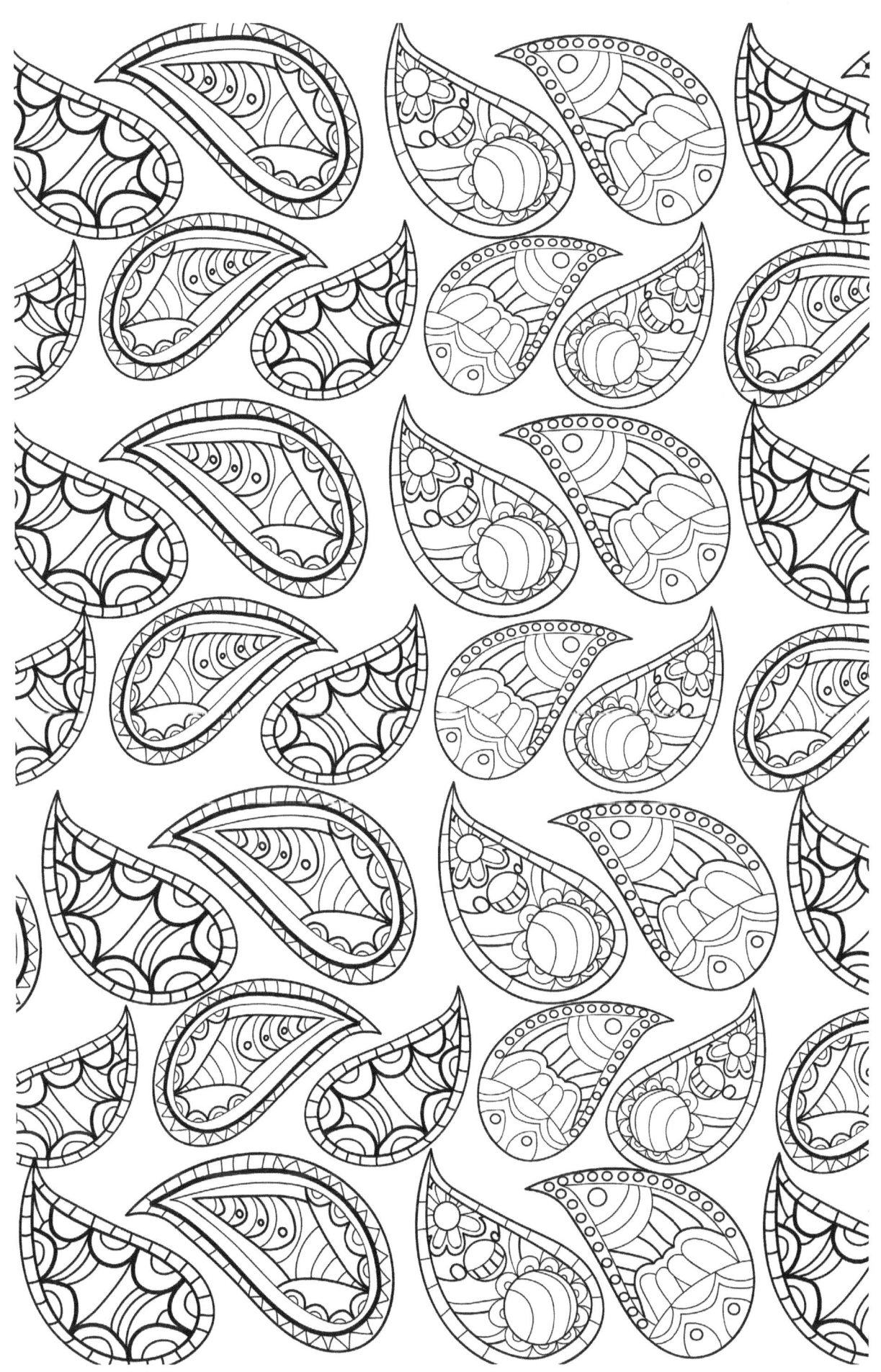

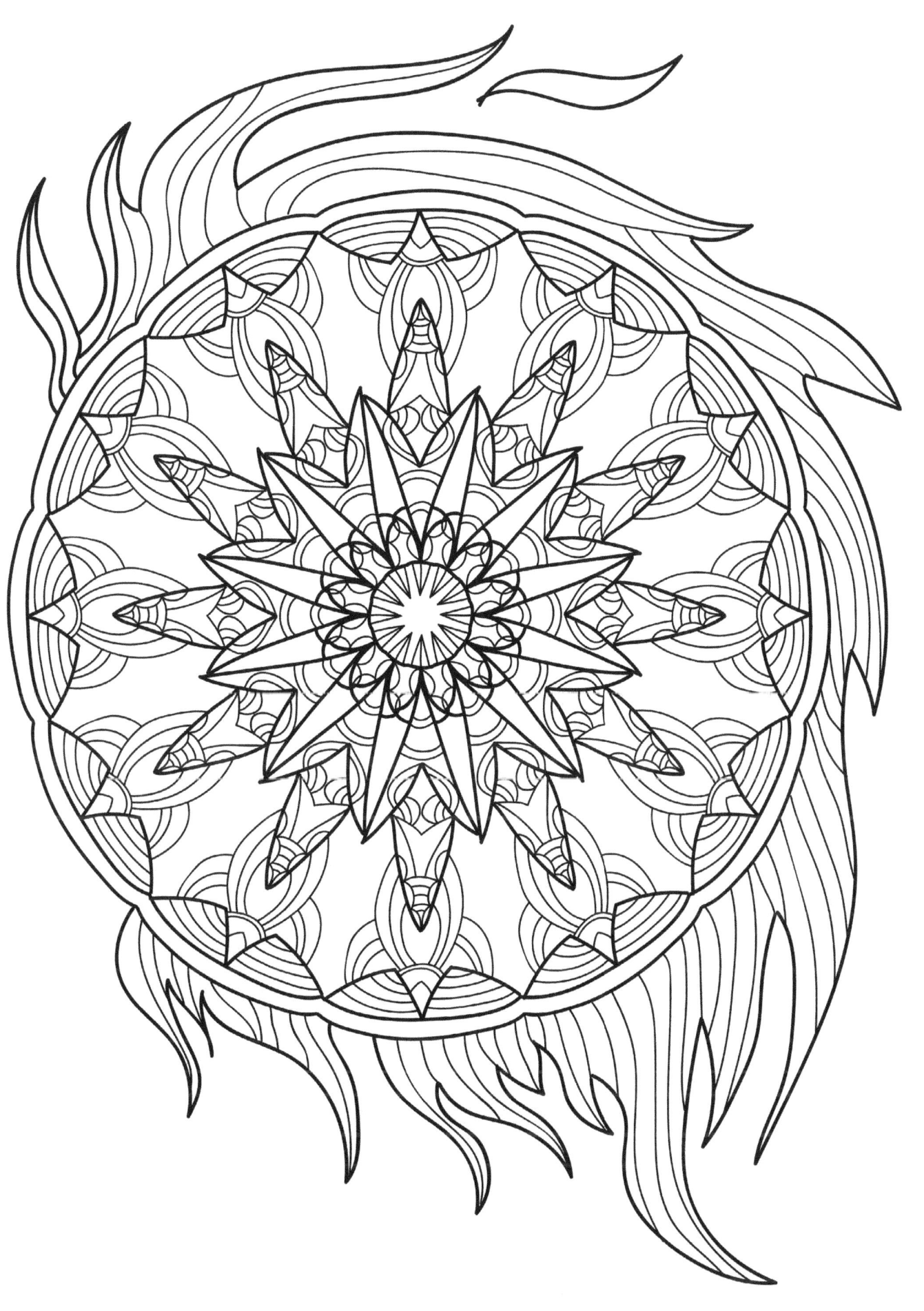

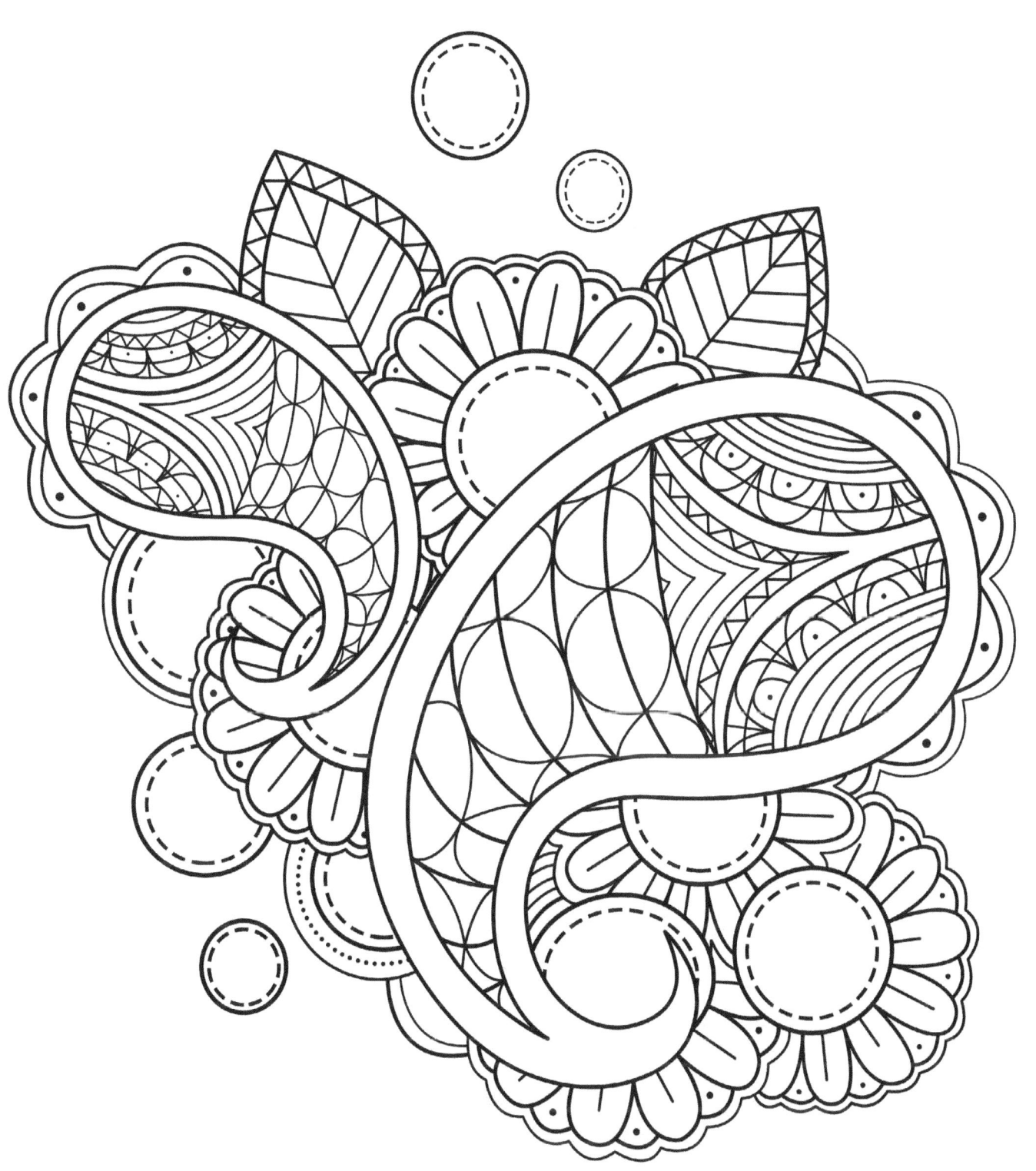

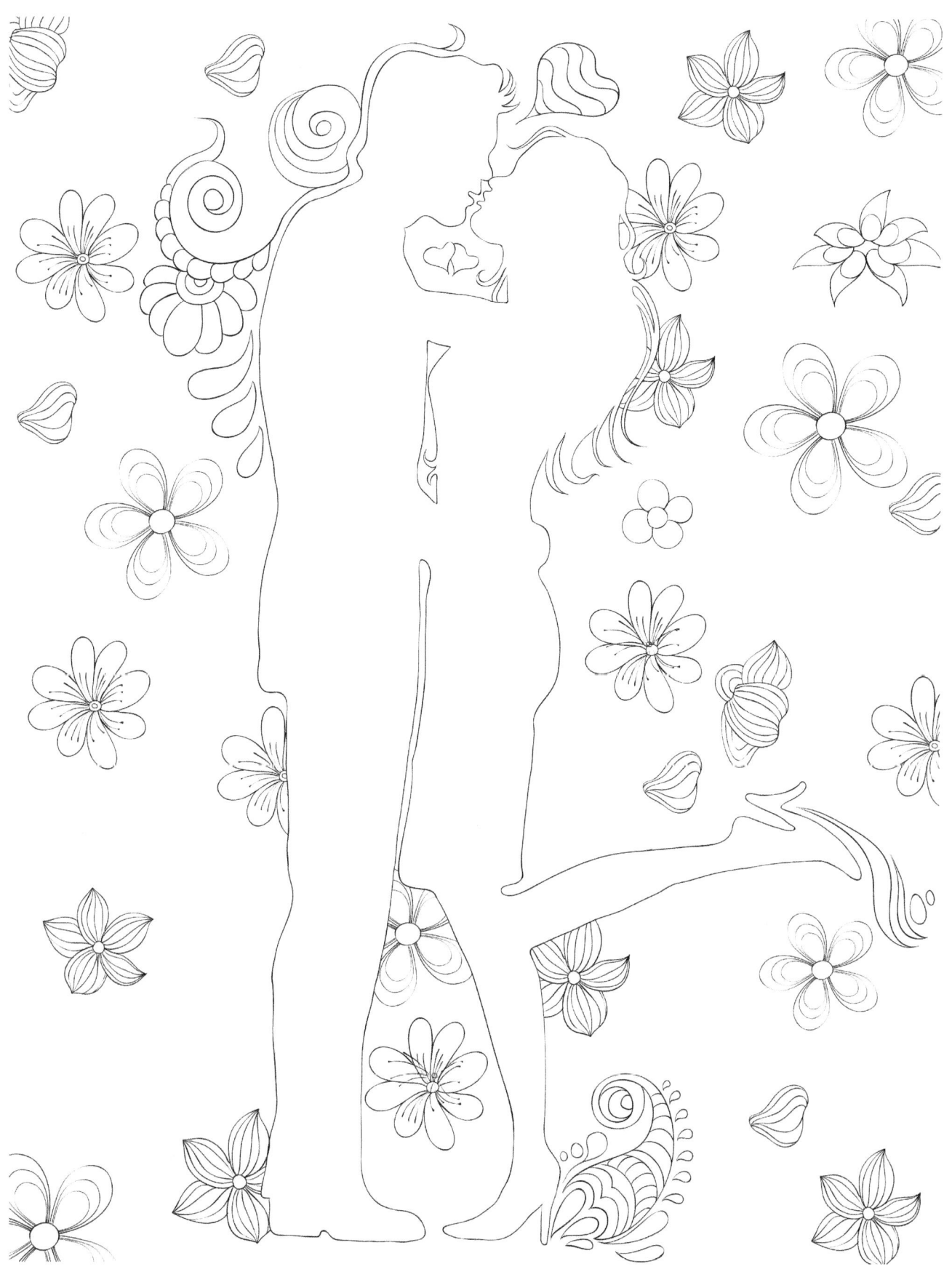

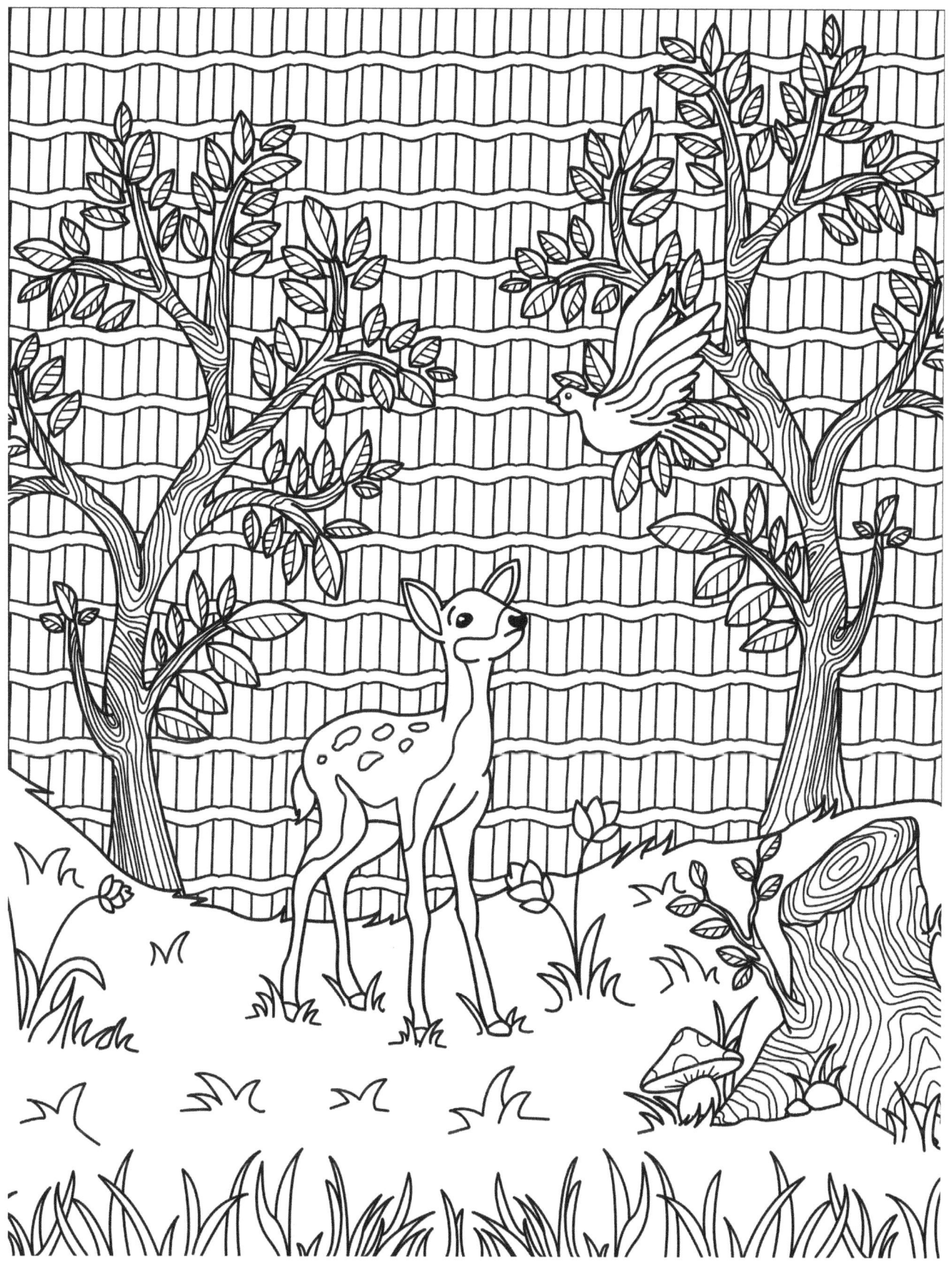

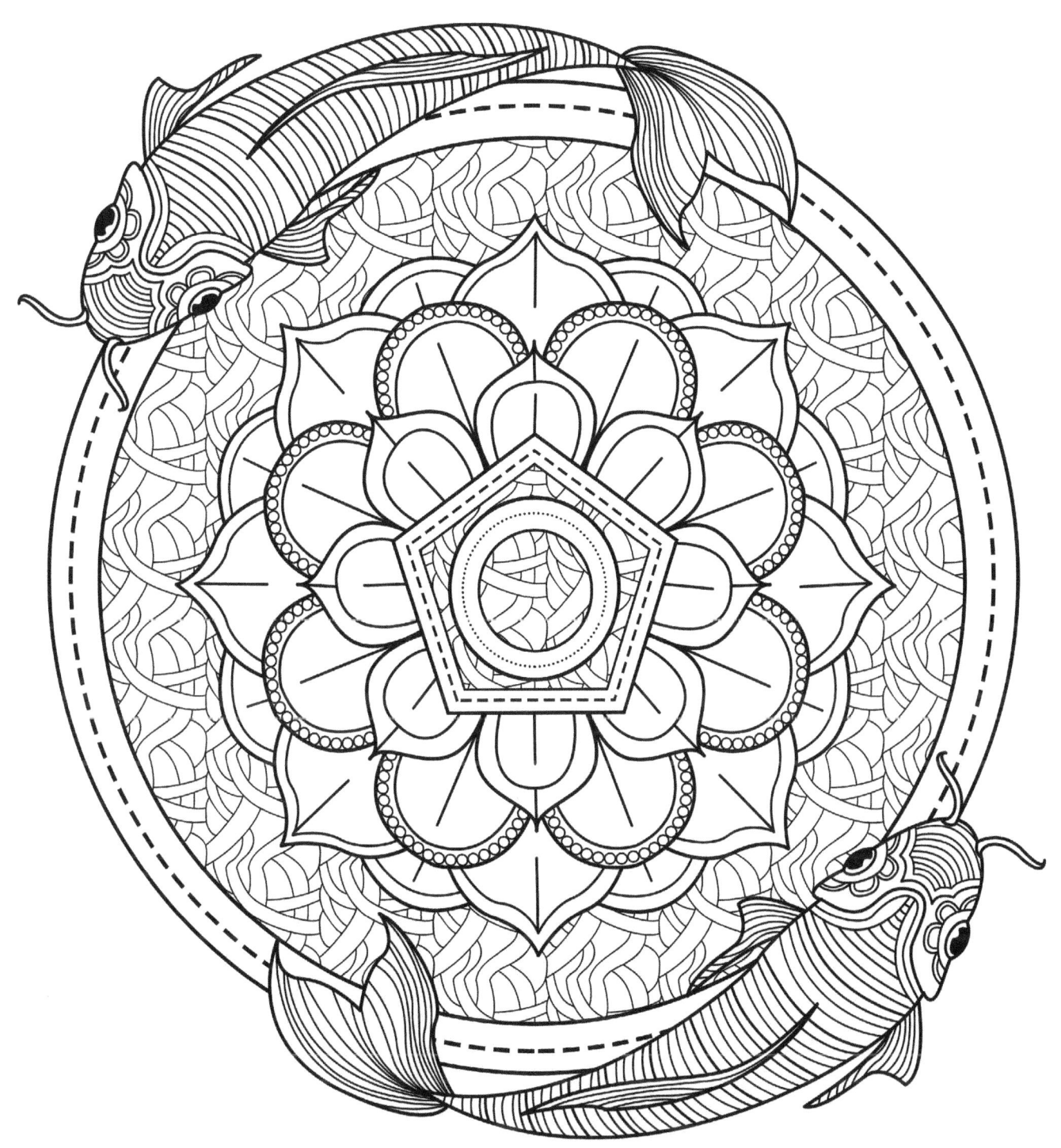

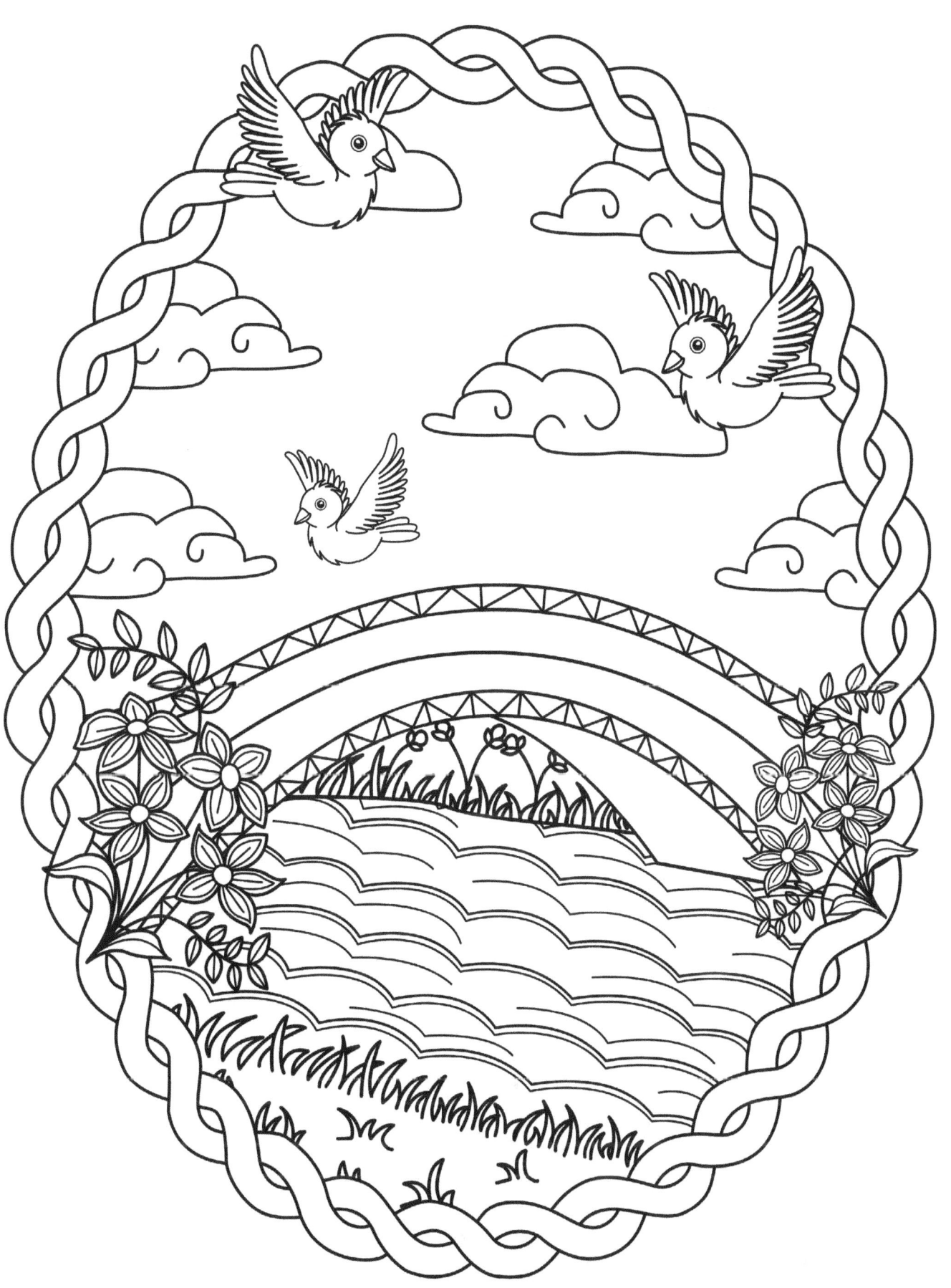

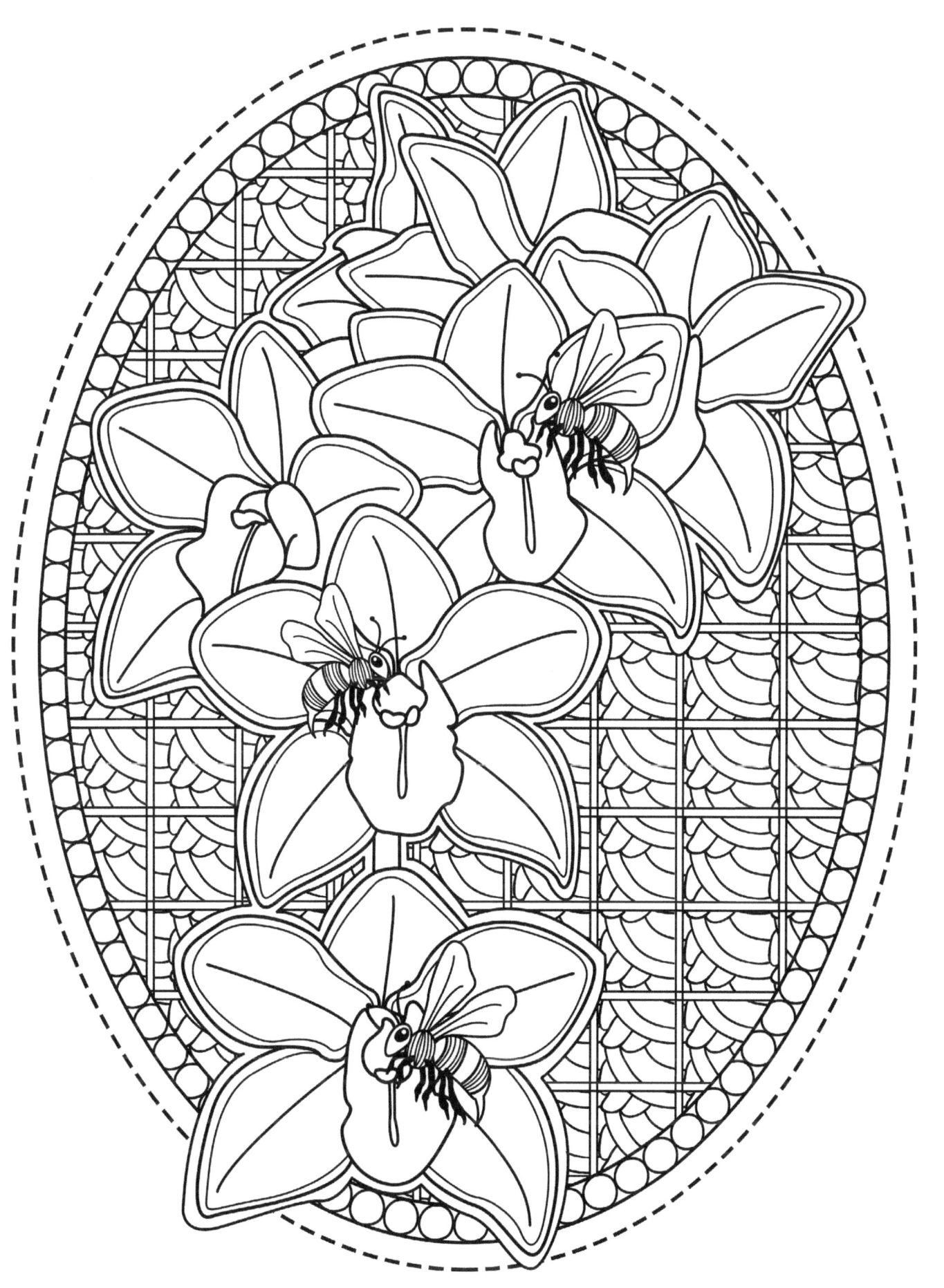

Free Bonus Book

$3.99 value electronic coloring book, easy to print out. Download your FREE book now:

http://CoolAdultColoringBooks.com

More: Check our website above for new books and special promotion deals…